Infosec Management Fundamentals

Infosec Management Fundamentals

Henry Dalziel

Contributing editor
Jerod Brennen

AMSTERDAM • BOSTON • HEIDELBERG • LONDON
NEW YORK • OXFORD • PARIS • SAN DIEGO
SAN FRANCISCO • SINGAPORE • SYDNEY • TOKYO

ELSEVIER

Syngress is an imprint of Elsevier

SYNGRESS.

Syngress is an imprint of Elsevier
225 Wyman Street, Waltham, MA 02451, USA

ISBN: 978-0-12-804172-7

British Library Cataloguing-in-Publication Data
A catalogue record for this book is available from the British Library

Library of Congress Cataloging-in-Publication Data
A catalog record for this book is available from the Library of Congress

For Information on all Syngress publications
visit our website at http://store.elsevier.com/

Working together
to grow libraries in
developing countries

www.elsevier.com • www.bookaid.org

CONTENTS

AUTHOR BIOGRAPHY

Henry Dalziel is a serial education entrepreneur, founder of Concise Ac Ltd, online cybersecurity blogger and e-book author. He writes for the Concise-Courses.com blog and has developed numerous cybersecurity continuing education courses and books. Concise Ac Ltd develops and distributes continuing education content [books and courses] for cybersecurity professionals seeking skill enhancement and career advancement. The company was recently accepted onto the UK Trade & Investment's (UKTI) Global Entrepreneur Programme (GEP).

CONTRIBUTING EDITOR BIOGRAPHY

Jerod Brennen (@slandail) by day is an infosec geek. By night, he's a husband, father, writer, filmmaker, martial artist, musician, gamer, and social media junkie. Jerod has earned every gray hair in his beard, having spent his career fulfilling infosec roles in higher education, consulting, retail, and public utilities. In that time, Jerod has worked on projects including security and compliance (GRC) program implementations, penetration tests, web and mobile application security assessments, and security tool deployments. Jerod shares what he's learned over the years with local and regional information security professional organizations, as well as attendees at larger information security conferences. He also teaches information security courses, both domestically and internationally. His approach to infosec has two key tenets: you shouldn't be afraid to void warranties, and you shouldn't need to bypass security to get your work done.

CHAPTER 1

Introduction

This book has been developed after gaining years of experience in a variety of IT and information security positions.

I progressed in my career from a level one (entry level) service desk employee to the CTO and Principal Security Consultant at a small information security consulting shop. In that time, in every role and position that I've worked in, the answers to my client's information security questions weren't instantly solved by the latest and greatest security tools; even in light of the latest attacks and techniques, everything that we're seeing in the information security space can be addressed and managed through some basic fundamental controls that we've known about for years. So, it's just having the knowledge, discipline, and "know how" to identify and implement those controls.

This book covers that information and will enable you to take that information back to your own organization and step into a leadership role.

Agenda

Scenarios

An ISO Approach

Key Strengths and Areas of Ownership

Resources

This book begins with a quick review of several scenarios, then it goes into a framework-based approach for implementing an information security program.

While the framework-based approach that I present builds on controls outlined in the ISO/IEC 27000 series, an internationally recognized body of standards for building out an information security management system (ISMS), you'll find that this same approach can be applied to any number of available frameworks.

Once we cover these details, we'll move on to building a security team by mapping key strengths to areas of ownership. Finally, I'll share resources that the more motivated security professional will want to investigate in order to further your understanding of the concepts presented here, and to dig deeper into specific areas of interest to you.

Where Are You Today?

You're not working in infosec yet, but you desperately want to move into that field.

You're a newly minted CISSP with your eyes on a position in infosec management / leadership.

You've recently accepted an infosec management / leadership position in a company that doesn't have an established (formalized) security program.

You've been in security management / leadership for years, and you want to take a step back and look at the entire program to determine whether or not you're covering all the bases.

You've recently made a move into consulting, and you want to ensure that your service offerings are appropriate for large enterprises and small / medium businesses.

Where are you today in your own information security career?

Perhaps you're not working in InfoSec yet, but you desperately want to move into this field. If that's so, good for you! That was the case with me a number of years ago. My background is actually in music education so when I went after my first IT security job, my resume did not reflect the education and training that someone would expect, which made it even more difficult me to land that role. The benefit that security-minded professionals have in today's market is that there in an ever-growing demand for information security professionals, with more open positions globally than job applicants.

Maybe you're a newly minted CISSP (Certified Information Systems Security Professional). Perhaps you've gone through the certification process, but you're in a more tactical operational role and you want to move into management. I spent years in that role at a large enterprise in Columbus, Ohio, developing my skills through hands-on opportunities to implement and maintain information security control systems. Don't underestimate the value of this hands-on experience!

It could be that you've accepted an information security management or leadership position. Now you've had this responsibility dropped on your lap, it's up to you to figure out what it means for your organization to be secure. That was my most recent enterprise position. This is where you learn to manage a security budget and a security team. This is also where most security professionals develop a much deeper understanding of the balance between business goals and information security controls.

It could be that you've been in that management or leadership role for years and you want to reverse your role, to step back as though you're looking from the outside and determine whether or not everything that you're doing is appropriate. Are you actually securing everything that needs to be secured? Is your security program complete and comprehensive? Is the value provided by your security program in-line with the goals of the business?

Finally, maybe you've made a move into information security consulting. You've had enough of the enterprise lifestyle and you want to take the expertise you picked up over the years and share that with other organizations so they understand where to start and how to implement security. Given the number of small and medium businesses at the root of every nation's economy, the sharing of your expertise in this fashion is of incredible significance!

Regardless of where you are today, the information we're about to cover is directly applicable to what you're doing. It's going to help you grow in your career. It's going to help you firm up a security program that you may be managing. The takeaway that I hope everyone gets from this material is that the information security field is in desperate need of motivated, dedicated professionals, individuals who, even if they don't yet have the background and experience, understand the importance and value of information security for businesses of all sizes. The variety of topics that we're about to cover—that knowledge is in high demand, and the information will help you find one of those open positions. More importantly, as anyone who follows the news knows, this knowledge is desperately needed.

Key Points About ISO 27k

International Standard
- Actually,16 standards
- 27000–27008, 27010–27011, 27031, 27033-1, 27044-1, 27035
- 27799: ISO27k for the healthcare industry

27001: Information technology—Security techniques—*Information security management systems—Requirements*

27002: Information technology—Security techniques—*Code of practice for information security management*
- *Fourteen categories of security management*

Formal Certification vs. Informal Adoption
- Your mileage may vary

I'm going to start with a framework, and while there are a number of frameworks available, the one that I personally have found the most success with is the ISO/IEC 27000 series.

You may be aware that ISO/IEC 27000 series is a collection of standards for implementing an information security management system (ISMS), but what most people don't realize is that the ISO/IEC 27000 series is actually 16 individual standards and documents. There's even a standard dedicated to implementing an information security management system in a healthcare organization (ISO/IEC 27799), where you are bound by Health Insurance Portability and Accountability Act (HIPAA) compliance and required to appropriately secure electronically protected health information (ePHI).

If you are just seeing the ISO/IEC 27000 series for the first time, ISO/IEC 27001 (Information technology—Security techniques—Information security management systems—Requirements) contains that core set of knowledge of information on what a program should look like. However, I have found the most value in focusing on the controls outlined in ISO/IEC 27002 (Information technology—Security techniques—Code of practice for information security controls).

I mentioned that I've worked in multiple enterprise information security roles. In one of those roles, I was brought into an organization to help them become Payment Card Industry Data Security Standard (PCI DSS) compliant. I learned very quickly that PCI compliance is a far cry from a comprehensive information security program, and I would argue that any of the numerous PCI-compliant organizations who have been breached recently would stand by me in that statement, understanding that they had likely gone through other stages of compliance, that they likely conducted penetration tests, but attackers were still able to find gaps in their security programs and defeat security controls, in some cases even eluding detection long enough to do significant damage. The PCI DSS was developed to address confidentiality first and foremost, in an effort to protect consumer credit card numbers, but does not pay equal attention to integrity controls, and it spends even less time addressing availability controls.

The ISO/IEC 27000 series, as opposed to something like PCI, goes into detail regarding specific controls designed to give you a strong, comprehensive information security control set. I've looked at Control Objectives for Information Technology (COBIT) from ISACA. While COBIT is an excellent framework in and of itself, the organization I was with at the time felt that may have been too formal, too regimented. I looked at the Information Technology Infrastructure Library (ITIL). For anyone working in a production control environment with high standards, the ITIL can help you ensure system uptime that meets customer service level agreements (SLAs), but ITIL is very light on information security.

The ISO/IEC 27002 control set, however, I found to be ideal. That said, when I approached my leadership about becoming ISO/IEC 27000 series certified, they disagreed with me and told me directly that was not the approach we were going to take. In retrospect, I agree wholeheartedly with that decision. The organization I was with did not have any financial benefit, any long-term benefit from having that certification. Simply put, the cost outweighed the benefit. However, an informal adoption of those controls significantly improved our information security program measurably from year to year. To the point that when I made the move from enterprise to consulting, I was very confident that individuals relying on the service my employer provided, and all the goods that we sold, would be delivered securely (both in person and online transactions).

In your role, that mileage may vary, you may be working for an organization where formal certification makes sense. However, if formal certification is not an option, you should still consider informal adoption as a viable alternative. I'll share some of why here in just a moment.

CHAPTER 2

ISO Security Management Categories

ISO Security Management Categories

Risk Management	
Policy Management	Security Operations Management
Security Organization Management	Communications Security Management
Human Resources Security Management	Systems Acquisition, Development, and Maintenance
Asset Management	Supplier Security Management
Access Management	Information Security Incident Management
Cryptography	Business Continuity Management
Physical and Environmental Security Management	Compliance Management

In 2013, the ISO/IEC 27000 series was updated to reflect a more refined control set. There are 14 categories identified in the standard, all of which fall under the umbrella of risk management.

- Policy Management
- Security Organization Management
- Human Resources Security Management
- Asset Management
- Access Management
- Cryptography
- Physical and Environmental Security Management
- Security Operations Management
- Communications Security Management
- Systems Acquisition, Development, and Maintenance
- Supplier Security Management
- Information Security Incident Management
- Business Continuity Management
- Compliance Management

Security controls are not one size fits all from one organization to the next. An organization that's very risk averse is going to be more locked down. They're likely going to implement a larger number of information security controls, and the quality of the controls they implement is going to be greater. However, they're also going to invest more time and resources into both implementing and maintaining those security controls, time, and resources that many smaller organizations don't have.

If you're working within a smaller organization, your leadership may be more willing to accept certain risks, more willing to take chances for the sake of competing and building out a customer base. Even smaller organizations will find value in these controls, but it's important for you to approach them with an understanding of the level of quality that is appropriate for your organization.

I found that a clearly defined approach to risk management, one where business leaders and security professionals openly discuss the bad things that could to happen and what steps the organization is willing to take in order to prepare for and respond when those bad things happen, is going to impact the control selection that you make from that ISO/IEC control set.

From Concept to Reality

Ask questions

Identify relevant controls

Build your checklist
- Starting point
- In the end, it's about trust and discipline

How do we get from this concept of a document, a published standard or framework to an actual implemented functional information security program? In my experience, it can be accomplished via a relatively simple process.

The first step (and this is very difficult for a number of IT folks, but we need to do it anyway) is to get out from behind our desks and ask questions. If you want to be successful in implementing an information security program you need to speak with people not only in IT, but in the business all throughout the organization. Throughout this material,

I'm going to give you guidance regarding questions you can ask in order to identify which controls are appropriate for your organization. Once you've had those discussions, that Q&A session, you're going to begin building a project list of controls that you've identified to be appropriate for your organization given your risk appetite. With that list in hand, you'll be able to discuss your desired level of quality, as well as project timelines for implementation activities. How soon do we need to make these changes? How much are we willing to spend? How many people do we need to support the changes?

That checklist that results from your discussions will be your starting point. It's from that checklist that you're going to drive all of the changes that you make. In the end, it's about the level of trust you're placing in your employees, your partners, and your suppliers, as well as the discipline that you, within your organization, are willing to adhere to in order to ensure that those controls are implemented and maintained.

Plan-Do-Check-Act (PDCA)

When implementing an information security controls framework, the Plan-Do-Check-Act model is incredibly appropriate. It worked extremely well in the organizations that I was working in.

In the "Plan" phase, you discuss which controls are relevant. You have the conversations, and you begin identifying changes that you intend to make in your organization in order to improve your security posture.

The "Do" phase is where those discussions transform into implementation projects. We develop project plans, we decide on project budgets, and we allocate resources who will actively spend time on implementing and maintaining these controls.

Once those projects are complete, once the controls have been implemented, you move onto the "Check" phase. This is where you validate whether or not the controls were implemented correctly. The IT Audit department plays a key role in this phase, as do external consultants.

I've worked with an organization who felt they had a terrific patching program in place and that they were doing an excellent job of identifying and remediating vulnerabilities. During one engagement, I discovered a critical (exploitable) vulnerability on one of the systems that stored sensitive information. When I presented this finding to the organization, they performed their own investigation and determined that the system fully patched and that my finding was incorrect. We were using different security tools and processes to evaluate technical vulnerabilities on the target system, and we disagreed over which finding was correct, and (more importantly) whether or not the vulnerability was even present. In the end, they found that there was a gap in their patch management program. It had deployed the patch to the target system, but hadn't appropriately installed the patch. A component of their patching solution had failed, and because they weren't checking whether or not the patches had been appropriately deployed, they had an exposure that could have potentially been exploited by an attacker. The "Check" phase where you revisit the controls after implementation and determine whether or not the control was appropriately implemented is incredibly important.

The "Act" phase, that fourth component of this cycle, is where you propose changes where you identify new controls (or perhaps controls that you hadn't yet discussed) and make proposals to implement those controls, which will take you back to the beginning Plan-Do-Check-Act model.

Of course, the model here is cyclical. It's intended to be a continuous process because information security is not a destination; it's a journey. At no point will you achieve at an absolutely secure set of controls, impervious to every attack. Threats will continue to evolve, as will attacks. If you follow bug bounty programs and competitions like Pwn2Own hosted at the CanSecWest security conference, you're aware of the economy that has grown around vulnerability discovery and disclosure. This economy is bringing more security researchers into the field and encouraging activity from independent researchers, which is contributing to a more rapid discovery and disclosure rate for technical vulnerabilities in critical systems. I would argue that may be why we're seeing attacks like Heartbleed, Shellshock, POODLE, Sandworm, VENOM, and so many critical vulnerabilities coming out each year. Even though our controls may have been initially implemented correctly and appropriately, the threat landscape has changed, as has the capability set of the attacker.

It's important for us to continually visit this Plan-Do-Check-Act cycle to ensure that the controls we've implemented are correct.

CHAPTER 3

Risk Management

Risk Management

Questions
- What could go wrong?
- How do our controls stack up?
- Are we spending a dollar to protect a dime?
- What's our risk appetite?

Controls
- Perform a risk assessment
  - Risk = Likelihood × Impact
  - NIST (800–30)
  - FAIR (Factor Analysis of Information Risk)

I mentioned that risk management is an umbrella under which all of these controls are identified and ultimately implemented. The first questions you should ask, and you can ask this of anyone, nontechnical or technical, are:

What could go wrong at our organization?
What are the bad things that can happen that we're worried about?

It's important that you have an open, honest conversation about the risks most likely to impact your organization, based on incidents that have happened within your industry, as well as incidents that may have happened within your organization in the past.

Once you begin identifying and articulating those concerns and fears, the next questions you should ask are:

How do our controls stack up?
If that bad thing were to happen, what defenses would we have to minimize damage?

Information security programs often grow organically, and you're likely to find that you already have some controls in place. Knowing where these controls have already been implemented will help you appropriately manage your information security budget going forward.

Once you've got the defenses and controls identified, the next logical questions are:

Are we spending too much?
Are we spending a dollar to protect a dime?

I've asked (and been asked) these questions many times throughout my career. Many organizations fall into the trap of making a gut feeling decision to implement a control, regardless of how much it costs, but if we approach our controls with a critical eye, we're likely to find that we're spending too much, that the amount of money we're spending on one control far outweighs the risk.

Finally, all of these questions are going to drive the final questions:

What's our risk appetite?
How much risk are we willing to accept?

As I mentioned earlier, security is not a one-size-fits-all solution for every organization. An organization that protects critical national infrastructure is likely to have a more conservative, more risk-averse appetite than an organization that sells t-shirts. Understanding your organization's risk appetite is essential if you want to be an effective information security manager.

The first control that I recommend every organization implement, a control that needs to be executed on a recurring basis, is some sort of risk assessment. If I look at the NIST Special Publication 800-30 revision 1 (Guide for Conducting Risk Assessments), they present a simple qualitative formula for calculating risk:

$$\text{Risk} = \text{Likelihood} \times \text{Impact}$$

Likelihood refers to how often a risk is likely to occur or be realized, and impact refers to how bad the damage would be if that were to happen. The NIST document provides additional recommendations on how to calculate the different scores.

If I wanted to go to the other end of the spectrum and look at a very quantitative approach to risk management, factor analysis of information risk (FAIR) gets into a very detailed comparison of the dollars and cents that an organization should be spending to manage identified risks. In my experience, performing a FAIR-based risk assessment requires more planning and training that performing a NIST-based risk assessment, but properly implemented, the FAIR methodology can provide very specific budgetary recommendations.

Regardless of whether you perform a qualitative NIST-based risk assessment, a quantitative FAIR-based risk assessment, or a risk assessment based on some other risk management methodology, that risk assessment will become the bedrock on which you build your information security program.

CHAPTER 4

Policy Management

Policy Management

Questions
- What rules do we expect our employees to follow?
- How do we do what we do?

Controls
- Policies, Standards, Procedures
  - Policy = Rules, high level
  - Standard = Technical requirements, detailed
  - Procedure = Step-by-step instructions
- Starting point = three <u>critical</u> policies
  - Information Security Policy
  - Data Classification Policy
  - Acceptable Use Policy
- If you want employees to know what's expected of them, you have to <u>write it down</u>!

Once you perform your risk assessment and you've begun the information security and risk management conversation started, the next step is to take a look at your information security policy set.

The questions to ask at this stage:

What are the rules that we expect our employees to follow?
If you are going to work at our company, what's okay and what's not okay?

For example, a very common question many companies are asking today is:

Should employees be allowed to bring their own personal devices (smartphones, tablets, etc.) and connect them to the internal wireless network?

Well, if you don't have a policy that clearly states what your rules are, then chances are people are going to do that without first seeking approval from someone in management. Documenting your expectations in policy is a crucial first step in mitigating these risks.

Once you've documented what's okay and what's not okay to do, with respect to your IT resources, you're going to begin addressing the next question:

How is it that we do what we do?

This shifts the conversation from high-level policies to more detailed standards and procedures. Let's continue with the personal device discussion. If your organization decides that the risk of allowing employees to connect personal devices to the company network is less than the cost of providing company-owned devices to those same employees, the security-minded manager asks questions about which controls are still necessary to implement for these users and their devices.

What does a secure iPhone look like?
What does a secure Android tablet look like?
Should we enforce passcodes or passwords?
Should we enable location services to locate lost or stolen devices, especially if that location tracking might violate employee privacy?
Is it okay to allow users to connect jailbroken iPhones and rooted Android tablets to our internal wireless network? (Hint: No. No it is not.)
What other security settings need to be turned on before we allow that phone to connect to our internal wireless network?

The specific settings that you insist users apply before connecting their devices to the internal wireless network should be documented in one or more standards. The process of actually changing those settings, however, would be a procedure. Procedures cover other scenarios as well.

What do we do (step-by-step) when someone leaves the company?
What changes do we make to their access?

Policies are very high level, they shouldn't change that often. Standards should be reflective of the technology, and as such should change as the technology changes. Continuing with the mobile example, every time a new version of iOS or the Android operating system is released, you should have a new standard regarding what a secure phone or tablet looks like within your organization. At the very least, you should publish a guideline with recommended settings that users should apply until the new standard has been developed, approved, and published.

Procedures will be used frequently by IT support teams. This is especially true for help desk and service desk teams, those parts of the IT organization that tends to function as the entry point for new employees. You should absolutely have detailed step-by-step instructions so that these teams can understand how to perform security tasks from the first day they start working with the company.

While a complete information security policy set can take some time to document, the three critical policies that I recommend everyone start with are:

1. Information Security
2. Data Classification
3. Acceptable Use

These three policies are just the tip of the iceberg, but they will help you quickly home in on how you do information security at you organization.

The Information Security Policy should identify the security rules that employees should follow. The Data Classification Policy should clarify the types of controls required for protecting more sensitive data, both at rest and in motion. (This policy is particularly important, as you'll learn later on, since there are many other policies, standards, and procedures that rely on that data classification policy.) Then, to address what actions are employees allowed to take while using company resources (namely Internet, email, mobile devices, and wireless networks), you'll want to document your Acceptable Use Policy.

If you want your employees to know what's expected of them, you have to write it down.

Otherwise you're destined to fail.

CHAPTER 5

Security Organization Management

Security Organization Management

Questions
- Who's going to do all this?

Controls
- Executive Sponsorship
- Information Security Steering Committee
- Information Security Team
  - Internal vs. External (NDA!)
  - Matrixed

With these policies in place, the next question you're going to ask is:

Who is going to do all this anyway?

I've heard the term unfunded mandate more than once, and I've been on the receiving end of that term where there was a new direction, a new rule that we're expected to comply with, regardless of whether or not we have the technology or staff to do so. The end result is often a new system deployed, but no designated admin.

This is where the concept of executive sponsorship, ownership of security from a C-Level executive, is critical. You need someone who can make budgetary and staffing decisions to support the policies that you've implemented. With the support of that executive sponsor, you should form an information security steering committee, a group of leaders within the organization to talk about how security changes impact their specific areas, and to help them collectively come to decisions regarding which controls you'll implement.

You'll also need an information security team, whether it's formed from internal staff or by engaging a third party managed security services provider. Someone will need to patch your systems. Someone will need to run vulnerability scans, to track your compliance status, to identify and remove instances of malware.

Make sure if you do have that external team in place, you document a nondisclosure agreement (NDA). You don't want your internal security incidents becoming public knowledge as part of that relationship.

I have also seen success with matrixed security teams, where organizations have a very small full-time information security resource or team, but then will engage people throughout IT and throughout the business to help out with security, even though those individuals are not full-time security professionals.

These three controls here will help you define and manage how you're going to run your security program.

CHAPTER 6

Human Resources Security Management

Human Resources Security Management

Questions

- Do we have job descriptions for the security team?
- Do our employees really know what's expected of them?
- Should we be doing background checks or credit checks on any employees?

Controls

- Job Descriptions
  - Manager, Senior Analyst, Analyst
- Non-Disclosure Agreement (NDA)
- Security Awareness Training
- Onboarding and Separations Procedures

Human Resources (HR) security management, our next category, focuses on job descriptions and training. Key questions related to this category include:

Do you have job descriptions for your security team?

If you were to go hire a new security team member, what title would you look for? What skills would you request?

Answering these questions is essential if you intend to find the right people for those roles, whether as internal employees or as third party managed security services providers.

Another crucial question:

Do your employees really know what is expected of them?

It's one thing to document this information in policy, but have you validated whether or not your policies are being adhered to?

One additional question that I feel you should ask when discussing human resources security controls is:

Should we be doing background checks or credit checks on any employees?

If someone is going to have access to highly sensitive information, you may want the peace of mind in knowing that they haven't had any criminal activity in their background, or that they're not in a financial compromised position. Knowing that the three common aspects of a crime are means, motive, and opportunity, you can reduce the risk of insider fraud by taking motive off the table.

Among the controls you would implement in this category are three key job descriptions:

1. An information security manager;
2. A senior security analyst; and
3. A security analyst.

I'll discuss these three roles in detail later on, but rest assured that they are critical elements of your information security control set.

As I mentioned earlier, a non-disclosure agreement (NDA), is another key control. This is often a boilerplate document that you can share with third parties to ensure that, if you choose to engage them in a way that requires the exchange of sensitive information, they are not going to disclose key internal information about your organization to anyone.

Security awareness training is another essential HR security control, not only for employees, but also for your IT staff to understand. If you want your employees to successfully detect and appropriately respond to social engineering attacks, teach them what an attack looks like and tell them who to contact when they are targeted. It's unreasonable to expect your developers to create secure web and mobile applications if you haven't taught them how to write secure code? Likewise, don't expect your system administrators to understand how to harden a Windows server or Linux server unless you've trained them.

Reiterating what I mentioned earlier in the policy section, onboarding and separations procedures are very important.

How do we hire someone and grant them access to internal systems? How do we end someone's time with our organization and take that access away?

These four HR security controls here will help you ensure that your information security control set is reasonable and appropriate.

CHAPTER 7

Asset Management

Asset Management

Questions
- What information assets do we have?
- How do systems enter the organization?
- What do we do with retired systems?

Controls
- Asset Tracking System
  - Discovery
  - Inventory
- Technology Purchase Request Form

In the asset management category, the key question we ask here is as follows:

What information assets do we have?

Put another way, do you know what systems are connected to your internal network? Because if you don't, it may not be prudent to consider it your network. Someone may have added a wireless access point or a rogue system that they are using to monitor employee activity, to access trade secrets, or to serve up malware to unsuspecting visitors to your website.

The threat of unmanaged devices and applications can come from within an organization as well. Departments with discretionary spending authority might purchase and implement a technology solution without ever engaging (or even notifying) the IT department. Gartner has coined the term "Shadow IT" to cover this.

What information assets do you have and how do you add systems to the network?
How do you acquire new technology?

Understanding how you acquire systems and applications and introduce them to your internal network is essential if you want to mitigate the risks associated with unmanaged technology.

Another key question:

What do we do with retired systems?
No piece of technology is going to last forever, and eventually you are going to turn it off. Take old hard drives for example. How many IT teams remove old hard drives and put them in a locked closet, a process that they will continue to follow until the closet is full? Storing old hard drives may be an acceptable solution for some organizations, depending on their risk appetite, until the closet is full. What do you do at that point?

Ask these questions, and you'll identify a need for some sort of asset tracking system where you can ideally discover all the systems on your network and then track that inventory as it changes over time.

In order to select the right asset tracking system for your organization, you need to know what information you need to collect about your systems. With mobile devices, a mobile device management (MDM) or enterprise mobility management (EMM) solution might contain pre-configured technical policies designed to collect information that most organizations have agreed is relevant. With workstations, you may already have a technology in place that is pushing software changes and patches to systems that does that tracking. You might use the same solution to patch and manage servers, although some organizations choose to manage their workstation population and their server population using different solutions.

Finding one centralized asset management system could be tricky for your organization, especially if you are budget-constrained. At the very least, a small organization with a spreadsheet that includes the DNS and IP address of every system on their network is a key control.

Also, in order to combat Shadow IT, a technology purchase request form can help you respond to departments or units within the organization who are purchasing systems or applications without checking with IT first. If you provide them with a way to acquire these solutions in a manner that keeps IT in the loop, IT might be able to help them better articulate their requirements and select an even more effective solution, not to mention a solution that adheres to your internal information security policies.

CHAPTER 8

Access Management

Access Management

Questions
- ○ Does everyone have access to what they need in order to do their jobs?
- ○ Can unmanaged devices attach to our network?

Controls
- ○ Principle of Least Privilege
- ○ Centralized User Directory
- ○ Access Reviews
- ○ Password Management
- ○ Lock Screens
- ○ Multi-Factor Authentication
- ○ Port Security

Access management deals with what resources people can get to, those resources they need in order to do their jobs. The first question you should ask is:

Does everyone have the access they need in order to do their jobs?

If someone starts a new job and they need to grant that person rights in Active Directory, a higher risk approach is to look at the most senior member of the company and say just copy his/her credentials. I say this is a higher risk, since it comes with a greater likelihood that you will potentially grant the new hire unnecessary access to systems that store sensitive data. If you provide people with the appropriate access they need in order to do their jobs, it's unlikely they are going to have a need or desire to circumvent your access controls (i.e., ask someone to share his/her username and password), but you first need to understand what those access rights are.

Another question you should ask:

Can unmanaged devices attach to our network?

Look at access management not from a user perspective, but from a device perspective. If someone can enter a conference room and plug an unmanaged laptop into a network jack, you have an exposure. If someone can connect a non-company wireless device to your wireless network, whether it is a laptop, a smartphone, or a tablet, they could potentially do a considerable amount of damage to the internal organization through that connection.

By asking those questions, you'll begin to identify the appropriate access rights for employees and networked devices, which is fundamental if you are to adhere to the principle of least privilege. Approaching every firewall rule, every Active Directory group, with the notion that we are only going to give people and systems just enough access to do what they need to do, is going to help you prevent both intentional and unintentional security incidents.

Some sort of centralized user directory is considering a leading practice in this area. Most often we see Active Directory from Microsoft, but directories such as OpenLDAP or eDirectory can often accomplish the same goal. Secure organizations need a central user store that all the systems can reference so that when someone is let go from an organization, an administrator can update that user's employment status in one place, and then the centralized directory can cut off that user's access immediately for all connected systems and applications. This control is especially important if the separation was unfriendly.

Access reviews are more of a procedure, albeit an important one, where you assign business managers (not IT managers) the responsibility of reviewing who has access to their systems and data, and then have them determine whether or not that access is appropriate. IT is never going to know with absolute certainty who should have access to what, but the line of business managers should. Performing these access reviews will help identify situations where the principle of least privilege is being violated, including violations that an automated system may have missed.

As much as I hate passwords as a security control, password management is still important. Identifying password length, password rotation requirements, the construction and complexity of passwords, and centralizing that functionality to ensure that strong passwords are in place across the entire organization has value. It's also important to ensure that password security controls are enforced through lock screens that time out, not only on workstations and laptops, but also on smartphones and tablets. Also included in this control set is a lock-out after a period of inactivity and the requirement for multi-factor authentication to systems that process and/or store sensitive data.

To clarify, multi-factor traditionally includes a combination of something you know, something you have, and something you are. Any combination of those two is going to make it much more difficult for an attacker to bypass a login screen. Mobile devices that have location services enabled allow for an additional factor of authentication (namely, somewhere you are).

Finally, access management can include network port security controls. If you have network jacks in conference rooms that no one's using, turn them off. If you have jacks underneath desks that aren't in use, turn those off as well. As long as you are only enabling ports where you have an active system connected, you are reducing the attack surface where someone could introduce an unmanaged device to your internal network.

Cryptography

Questions
- Do we encrypt sensitive data at rest?
- Do we encrypt sensitive data in motion?

Controls
- Documented Encryption Policy
- Documented Encryption Key Management Procedures
- SSL/TLS Encryption
- Hard Drive Encryption
- Database Encryption
  - Cell vs. Row vs. Table

The conversation about cryptography (or encryption) controls begins by asking two basic questions:

Are we encrypting sensitive data at rest?
Are we encrypting it while it's in motion?

We've seen a shift in the industry, and it's really picked up steam as of late, to "encrypt all the things." If you have something that you want to protect, putting encryption in place is a great way, arguably, to do that. I say arguably, because encryption requires disciplined encryption key management practices. Anyone who has been impacted by a ransomware such as CryptoLocker or CryptoWall can attest to the harm caused by an encrypted file system where the decryption key is unavailable. The controls that you identify as a result of this conversation should be documented in your encryption policy, as well as in your encryption key management procedures.

Discussions around encrypting network traffic most often steer toward properly implemented SSL and TLS, although the informed information security manager is aware of critical vulnerabilities in certain encryption mechanisms (POODLE being the one that comes to mind right away). It's not enough to just "encrypt" the data. Encryption controls must be securely implemented and constantly monitored for new vulnerabilities.

When it comes to encrypting hard drives, whole disk encryption is considered a leading practice. Before you can encrypt your hard drives, however, you need to ask some specific questions.

What technology are you going to use?
How are you going to manage the encryption keys?
Is the encryption mechanism vulnerable to bypass attacks?
Do you need the ability to centrally manage encryption keys?

When considering encryption at the database level, it is especially important to take performance impacts into account. That said, database encryption of some sort is another recommended control, since databases tend to be repositories of critical information.

Are we going to encrypt data at the cell level, or are we going to encrypt at the row level?
Are we going to encrypt entire tables?

Fine tuning that encryption so that you are protecting the sensitive, most critical data, without disrupting business processes (i.e., doing more harm than good) is key.

CHAPTER 10

Physical and Environmental Security Management

Physical and Environmental Security Management

Questions
- What's our perimeter?
- Could someone walk into any of our locations and take something that doesn't belong to them?

Controls
- Locks
  - Sensitive areas
- Badges
  - Employee, Contractor, or Visitor?
- Physical Security Assessment

The area of physical and environmental security management surprised me the most when I initially implemented my first information security program. I must admit, I didn't fully understand the role in physical security played by the information security manager.

A few key questions:

What is your physical perimeter?
Can someone walk into your server room and steal the system?
Can someone walk into an office location and take a smartphone, a tablet?
Can someone get into a network device closet and plug something into a switch?
What is your perimeter and can someone take away something that does not belong them?

As you can imagine, many of the logical security controls you choose to implement are at a greater risk of compromise if you lose physical control of the devices you are trying to protect.

Locks around sensitive areas are an excellent control—locks, I should clarify, that can't easily be bypassed with a bump key or a modified hotel key card. As anyone who has followed Chris Nickerson's exploits is aware, a clever attacker can compromise sophisticated systems like motion detector locks with a Mylar balloon and a warm wash cloth, tricking the system into thinking it is sensing a living person.

Understanding the attacker will help you understand what locks are appropriate for your organization. Providing badges, some sort of identification for employees so you can just distinguish an employee from a contractor from a temporary visitor, is also important from a security awareness perspective, especially if you encourage your employees to challenge (or offer to assist) anyone wandering around a sensitive area without a visible badge.

Doing some sort of physical security assessment will also help you better understand your exposures in this area. Dumpster diving can help you determine whether or not sensitive information is being thrown away without being shredded. Hiring someone to actually try to break into one of your offices is another excellent test. This is particularly important for remote locations, locations far enough from headquarters that security controls may not be actively enforced.

All of these controls will go a long way to address the associated physical and environmental risks.

CHAPTER 11

Security Operations Management

Security Operations Management

Questions
- Who's responsible for the day-to-day security stuff?
- What exactly is the day-to-day security stuff?

Controls
- Security Operations Procedures
  - Change Control
- Antimalware
- Encryption
- Logging and Monitoring
  - Enabled, centralized, and detailed

When considering security operations management, your administration of the day-to-day security tasks, the following question comes to mind:

Who is responsible for the day-to-day security stuff?

We talked about security organization management earlier. Now, we take it a step further, because when we are talking about who's responsible for the day to day security, we also have to ask:

What exactly is the day to day security "stuff"?

Log reviews, running vulnerability scans, patching systems, responding to potential security incidents ... the day-to-day responsibilities of an information security team can be considerable. Once you have identified all of those procedures, you're going to be able to identify who is (or who should be) responsible for managing them.

Security operation procedures include repeatable tasks such as change control. Often times, unauthorized changes can be more damaging to a system then an external attacker, so your change control procedure is a key control in the security operations management category. Management of end point security agents, which might include antimalware and/or desktop encryption, also fall into this category.

Logging and monitoring is another key control that falls under security operations management. While it is important that we make every effort to prevent bad things from happening, it is also important that we have the ability to detect when they have happened so that we can respond to them very quickly. You can accomplish this by implementing a centralized logging mechanism that is gathering logs from all of the systems that you need to watch and capturing enough log data that you could perform both near real-time alerting of security incidents as they occur, as well as the more long-term investigation of security incidents and their root causes, tasks that we often associate with the field of computer forensics.

CHAPTER 12

Communications Security Management

Communications Security Management

Questions
- Have we segmented our networks based on our information classification policy (i.e., principle of least privilege)?
- Have we appropriately secured all data exchanges with third parties?

Controls
- Network Segmentation
- Firewall Security Audits
- System-to-System Encryption
- Contracts, Confidentiality Agreements, & NDAs

Communications security management deals primarily with network security controls.

One key control is network segmentation, so the first question I would ask is:

Have we segmented our networks based on our information classification policy?

You'll remember previously that I recommend three critical policies, and that the data classification policy is one of them. You'll find it very difficult to restrict access to sensitive data unless you know how your organization classifies data, where that sensitive data resides, and who has access to it. Once you've done that classification and segmented your network, it's going to make it a lot harder for an attacker to get to that data without legitimate access.

You should also ask the question:

Have we appropriately secured all data exchanges with third parties?

I guarantee that you are doing business with at least one third party today, most likely a cloud service provider, and the question you should ask from the security management perspective is:

How do we take in the appropriate action to lock down that communication to ensure that unauthorized third parties can't access the information we're exchanging with the authorized third party?

When implementing network segmentation, it is important that you first consider the level of complexity that your network administration team can reasonably support? I've visited organizations where I've logged on to their public (unencrypted) guest wireless network and had direct network access to patient and billing systems. From a security perspective, that is a terrible network architecture design, but they didn't design the network with security in mind. Their first priority was simplicity. They hadn't had the discussion with their security team around network segmentation and therefore had a huge exposure.

Firewall security audits are another key control. Reviewing the rules to determine how an outsider, for example, might be able to follow a network path to an internal system or location. Do you have any exposures or gaps there? If you do, perhaps it's time to consider system-to-system encryption where you encrypt data even on the internal network. An internal (unencrypted) FTP process from one server to another may seem secure because it's on the inside, but once an unauthorized party gains access to the internal network, you now have both credentials and potentially sensitive data exposed in plaintext.

In addition to these technical controls, documentation controls such as security language in contracts, confidentiality agreements, and NDAs with your third parties will help ensure that they are following the rules that you've laid out.

CHAPTER 13

Systems Acquisition, Development, and Maintenance

Systems Acquisition, Development, and Maintenance

Questions
- How do we secure new systems before we add them to our network?
- Do we have production data in nonproduction systems?

Controls
- System hardening process
- Software Development Lifecycle (SDLC)
- Change control procedures
  - Change Approval Board (CAB)
- Vulnerability management procedures
  - Development, QA, Production
  - Scan <u>EVERYTHING</u> (hosts, databases, apps)
  - Penetration testing (validate your controls)

Systems acquisition, development, and maintenance—what question do we ask here?

How do we secure new systems before we add them to our network?

We're bringing new systems and new applications online all the time, but we can't assume that they've all been properly locked down.

Do we have production data in nonproduction systems?

I still see this today, and I understand why. Developers are moving quickly, constrained by limited budgets and tight project deadlines, and they need to test their applications with a high degree of accuracy. It's difficult to come up with test data that is as accurate of a reflection of production as actual production data. That said, I've been in organizations doing internal penetration tests where I've been able to compromise sensitive production data sets by exploiting weaknesses on the nonproduction systems where that data had been stored during the testing process (and, unfortunately, subsequently forgotten). This was possible because those nonproduction systems didn't have the same level of security and control as the production systems, a condition that is true in many organizations.

A handful of controls you can implement to address risks associated with systems acquisition, development, and maintenance are documented system hardening procedures, a secure software development lifecycle, and change control procedures that include an approval board tasked with reviewing all changes before they're implemented to ensure that those changes don't inadvertently or break anything.

Vulnerability management procedures also fall under this category, which includes scanning development, test, quality assurance (QA), and production systems for exploitable technical vulnerabilities. If an attacker compromises a nonproduction host system, even if that system is devoid of production data, that attacker can still use that host as a jump point to get to other host systems. Alternately, the attacker may use that access to execute a pass-the-hash attack, which could be particularly devastating if domain admin credentials are stored locally on that nonproduction system.

Don't just scan host systems, though. Scan your databases. Scan your applications. Bear in mind that the tools most commonly used to detect host-level vulnerabilities are not always the same tools that will inform you of critical database- or application-level vulnerabilities. Here's a good rule of thumb: If an attacker can interact with a resource, it's on the security manager to figure out how to identify and mediate any vulnerabilities that may be present in that resource.

Once you have vulnerability scanning and remediation well in-hand, penetration testing is the next valid step. Penetration testing is a method for validating whether or not the controls you've implemented are actually effective in deterring an attacker. A vulnerability scan is going to tell you that you have critical exposures. A penetration test is going to help you understand whether or not an attacker might actually be able to take advantage of that exposure, exploit it, and either access sensitive data or cause a business disruption.

CHAPTER 14

Supplier Security Management

Supplier Security Management

Questions
- Who are all of our suppliers?
- Do they know our security (and compliance) expectations?

Controls
- Supplier List (Accounting)
- Documented Supplier Information Security Requirements
- Contracts, Confidentiality Agreements, & NDA's
- Supporting Procedures
  - Supplier Information Security Assessment
  - Supplier Information Security Audit

Supplier security management has become more and more important as of late, especially when it was revealed that attackers were able to compromise Target customer data in 2013 by first compromising one of Target's suppliers, and then exploiting that supplier's access to install malware on internal Target systems.

Ask your organization these questions:

Who are all of our suppliers?
Who are the third parties with whom we exchange information?

What you'll find when you ask these questions is that that list is going to continue to grow and grow with every person with whom you speak. With the advent of cloud computing, we have more and more third parties who offer critical business services and apps that our internal users increasingly rely on. You'll find that many business units have already engaged these third parties without IT's knowledge, as I mentioned earlier.

Who are these suppliers?
Who are these third parties and do they know our security and compliance expectations?

PCI, the payment card industry, clearly states that if you are sharing credit card data with any third party, then that third party must also demonstrate PCI DSS compliance. Do your suppliers know of this responsibility? Have you told them?

One of the key controls that is going to become apparent after you've asked these questions is a documented list of your suppliers. I've found that the best way to compile this list is to follow the money. Speak with your accounting department. They should be able to provide you with the majority of the list, because if you are engaged with a third party for business, you are either paying them money or they are paying you. That exchange of money is being tracked somewhere. If you can get into the system that is tracking that list of exchanges, you'll have your list of suppliers.

You should also have a documented supplier information security requirements checklist of some sort.

What information security expectations do you have of them?
Do they have to adhere to PCI?
Do they have to adhere to HIPAA?
Do they have to adhere to the SANS 20 Critical Security Controls, or does it make more sense for them to adhere to Common Sense Security Framework?

Your organization needs to agree on the security controls that suppliers and partners must have in place, and then someone must own the responsibility of communicating those controls to the necessary parties.

Contracts, confidentiality agreements, and NDA's come up here again, in addition to two key supporting procedures: a supplier information security assessment and a supplier information security audit. You need to be able to quickly assess whether or not they have key controls in place, but in some cases you'll need to dig deeper and ask them to provide evidence. That's where the audit comes into play.

CHAPTER 15

Information Security Incident Management

Information Security Incident Management

Questions
- What could go wrong?
- What's already gone wrong?
- What do we do when something goes wrong?

Controls
- Security Incident Response
  - One Policy
  - Many Procedures
- Security Information Event Management (SIEM) System
- Training
  - End User Security Awareness
  - Incident Response
  - Forensics
- Tabletop Exercises

Information security incident management is the next category.

Returning to that risk discussion, the umbrella under which all these controls are discussed, a pair of more in-depth questions arise:

What are the things that could go wrong?
What are the things that have already gone wrong?

As we have matured in detecting and responding to security incidents, we now have some data that we can go back to. For example, let's say that your organization has been tracking the number of lost and stolen laptops and mobile devices reported annually, as well as the number of service desk calls where a support technician had to manually remove malware from an end user's machine. Worst case scenario, perhaps your organization actually saw a data breach. By analyzing all of this data, you can improve your security incident detection and response capabilities.

Another key question:

When something goes wrong what do you do?

If the answer is, "We run around screaming with our hair on fire," then your organization definitely has an opportunity to improve this particular security control set.

If you document one security incident response policy with multiple supporting procedures, a procedure for each specific type of incident you plan to address, then you can plan ahead of time how to quickly contain the damage and prevent the incident from having a greater impact on your business.

A security information event management (SIEM) system is another critical control, although somewhat more advanced. Hopefully, you already have a centralized log management system collecting log data from network devices, critical host systems, and critical applications. A fine-tuned SIEM system could normalize and analyze that data, search for potential attack patterns, and then alert security staff when those patterns are detected.

Training comes up here again, reinforcing what we covered during the HR security management section. You should train your end users on how to detect and respond to security incidents, especially social engineering attacks. Teach them to never engage a social engineer. Teach them to always report social engineering to someone in security. The security team can then communicate to other areas of the business to be on the lookout for that type of attack. You should also train the incident response team on how to respond to incidents. Tabletop exercises are an excellent control that allow responders to simulate a response and detect potential gaps in their response procedures or in the controls that they have implemented to support security incident response activities.

Larger organizations may want to consider training staff in proper computer forensics techniques, especially if that data is ever going to be used in court. That said, many organizations find it to be much more cost-effective to maintain a relationship with a certified security provider who specializes in computer forensics.

CHAPTER 16

Business Continuity Management

Business Continuity Management

Questions
- How will we recover from a disaster?
- How will we keep the business going during the recovery process?

Controls
- Disaster Recovery Plan
- Business Continuity Plan
- Backups
- Tabletop Exercises

Business continuity management controls focus on helping you prepare for and recover from a disaster, as well as how you continue to operate during that recovery period.

The first question:

How will we recover from a disaster?

... is answered by your disaster recovery plan. This document outlines how you will bring your IT systems back online, how you will restore data, and in what order these events will occur. As you can imagine, generating and testing your backups on a regular basis is critical to this plan. You may be backing up data, but if you are not testing your backups, you may find during a security incident or a recovery event that your backups are useless or they've broken, that they've stopped backing up at some point and no one was monitoring. This is why tabletop exercises and mock recovery exercises are necessary.

The second question:

How will we keep the business going during the recovery process?

... is answered by your business continuity plan. This document differs from the disaster recovery plan, in that it focuses on how you will continue to operate securely while the disaster recovery efforts are underway.

CHAPTER 17

Compliance Management

Compliance Management

Questions
- What do I need to comply with?
  - HIPAA, PCI, NERC/FERC, SOX, COPPA, FERPA, CFPB, etc.
  - External <u>and</u> Internal

Controls
- Documented Compliance Procedures
  - Who is responsible for what?
  - When is it due?
- Unified Compliance Framework
- Audits
  - External <u>and</u> Internal
  - Scheduled, nonintrusive, and independent

The last group of security controls I want to cover fall under compliance management.

There are two key questions here:

What do I need to comply with?
What rules and regulations exist that apply to me?

HIPAA, PCI, NERC/FERC, SOX, COPPA, FERPA, CFPB ... the list is staggering. There are so many acronyms that identifying what's relevant to you can take a lot of time. Organizations such as the Unified Compliance Framework exist solely to track the hundreds of regulations that exist around the globe, and to help organizations make sense of the compliance process.

Keep in mind that you're looking not only at external compliance requirements, but also at internal policies that you've published. What do we need to comply with there? Having documented compliance procedures where you identify who is responsible for demonstrating compliance and when that evidence is due is important.

I've seen governance, risk, and compliance (GRC) solutions that track some of this information for you. GRC solutions help you track not only your organization's internal and external compliance obligations, but also the level of compliance that your suppliers have demonstrated with the information security requirements that you've shared with them.

Validating compliance often occurs during internal and external audits. Ideally, audits should be conducted in a manner that is both nonintrusive and independent.

Once you go through the process of asking questions related to the security controls that you've decided to implement, with respect to the risk appetite expressed by your leadership, you're now ready to step back and take a look at your information security program. You've got a picture, a framework, of what your security program should look like and how well your plan stacks up to the actual control set.

CHAPTER 18

Skillset Groupings

Skillset Groupings

Business (People)	Process	Technical (*ology)
Security Organization	Risk	Physical
	HR Security	Asset
	Business Continuity	Security Operations
	Security Incident	Acquisition and Development
	Policy	Access
	Compliance	Cryptography
	Supplier Security	Communications Security

This chart identifies <u>key strengths</u>, which align with <u>areas of ownership</u>.

Now we need to talk about who's going to do this. How do we put people in the right role?

What I have found is that if you group these areas of responsibility in the traditional People/Process/Technology matrix, here's how it breaks out.

You should have a business-minded person for security organization management. I only assign one area to the business person, but trust me when I say that having a person solely focused on the relationship between security and the business is a full-time job.

To the process-minded person, I would assign risk, HR security, business continuity, security incident, policy, compliance, and supplier security. While each of these areas have a technical component, the process of implementing and maintaining these controls takes precedent.

To the technical person, I would assign physical, asset, security operations, acquisition and development, access, cryptography, and communications security. This person will have to roll up his/her sleeves and get into the technical weeds when covering these specific areas.

This chart takes key strengths, identifying what people are good at, and then assigning those responsibilities to the right people. If you strive to always put somebody in a role where they are happy and they enjoy what they are doing, your information security program will be even more effective.

Business Skillset

"People person"

Information security governance

Compliance and regulatory knowledge

Understand integration points among business, security, and compliance

Managing people

(ISC)2 CISSP and/or ISACA CISM
  ○ Maybe even SANS Masters Degree in Information Security (MSISM)

For the business skillset, this is your people person. This is someone who understands information security governance, has compliance and regulatory knowledge and understands how business, security, and compliance all work together.

These people work well together with other people. They're good at managing teams, both technical and nontechnical.

If you were to use certifications to help you find the right candidate for this role, I would look for someone with their CISSP (from ISC2), their CISM (from ISACA), or perhaps even their MSISM from SANS.

Process Skillset

Accountant

Blend of business and technology

Policies, standards, procedures

Understanding of business process flows

ISACA CISA

The process skillset people are your accountants. They like numbers, they like tracking things, and they have a mix of business and technology skills. They love documentation; processes, procedures, and standards make their day. They also understand business process flows, a skillset often found in business analysts.

Here, I've found that Certified Information Security Auditors (CISAs) are a terrific fit for this role.

Technical Skillset

Geek/Nerd

System administration

Active in technical/security user groups

Deep knowledge of specific technologies

(ISC)2 CISSP + Specific tech certs

Your technical skillset will be found in your geeks and nerds, terms that I use with the utmost affection (being a geek myself). First and foremost, they have done system administration in the past. They're active in technical and security user groups and they have a deep knowledge of specific technologies.

If you're looking at resumes, these folks may or may not have their CISSP, but they are likely to have one or more technical certifications related to specific technologies.

Core Team

Manager
- Business-oriented, with understanding of tech and process
- The buck stops here
- Strategic

Senior
- Highly Technical and Process-Oriented, with business knowledge
- Primary and Secondary
- Strategic + Tactical

Junior
- Technical and Process-Oriented
- Primary and Secondary
- Tactical + Operational

Ideally, your core information security team that has three tiers: a manager, one or more senior security analysts, and one or more (junior) security analysts. The size of the team will vary, depending on the size of your organization and on any relationships you might have with third party managed security services providers. Regardless, the overall structure can still apply.

The business-oriented manager is responsible for strategic decisions, where the senior security analyst has strategic conversations with the manager and then translates that into tactical information when working with the junior security analyst.

Effective information security programs are driven by information security managers who encourages seniors to help the juniors grow into senior positions. The juniors should be constantly learning from the seniors, seeking new ways to improve existing processes based on that accumulated knowledge. This enables juniors to maintain operational day-to-day responsibilities until they grow into a senior, at which time you can hopefully bring new junior security analysts onto the time.

Sample Org Chart

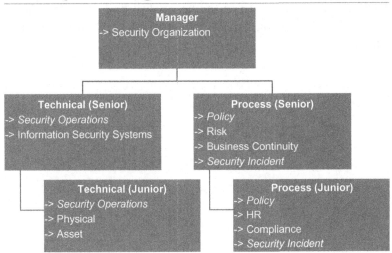

On the following slide, I've included a sample organization chart to show you how this all maps together.

The manager is responsible for securing the organization and if you have a team of four full time security professionals (which I know is a luxury for many organizations), you ideally would have a technical senior and a process senior who would have the responsibilities I have outlined here. Then each senior would have a junior who shares certain responsibilities. For example, the technical senior shares security operations with a technical junior, but the junior may be responsible for physical security and asset security where the technical senior may be responsible for that system acquisition in maintenance. Likewise, the process senior shares policy with the junior, but maybe the junior handles the awareness training for HR while the process senior handles all of the risk assessment.

Again, this is just a sample. Your organization doesn't need to look like this, but understand that if you start with a framework and identify in that risk-based context all of the controls that are relevant to your organization, the discussion around security organization and the operations management, around who is going to implement and maintain all of these controls, is ultimately going to lead to an organization chart where you can identify where those responsibilities lie.

When you are in that management role, you will also find that this is how you drive staffing changes. This is how you communicate to leadership that, in order to meet the quality or level of security outlined in your information security policies, you will likely need to have people in these roles.

CHAPTER 19

Resources

Resources

Wikipedia
- http://en.wikipedia.org/wiki/ISO/IEC_27001
- http://en.wikipedia.org/wiki/ISO/IEC_27002

International Organization for Standardization
- ISO/IEC 27001:2013
  - http://www.iso.org/iso/catalogue_detail?csnumber=54534
- ISO/IEC 27002:2013
  - http://www.iso.org/iso/catalogue_detail?csnumber=54533

The ISO 27000 Directory
- http://www.27000.org/iso-27001.htm

ISO 27001 Security <- GREAT starting point
- http://www.iso27001security.com/

As I mentioned at the beginning of the presentation, I am a strong advocate for sharing resources.

The first set that I wanted to share was around the ISO/IEC 27000 series. If you want to read up on the ISO 27001 and 27002, start with Wikipedia. In addition to being a free resource, it's been my experience that technical information on Wikipedia is often kept up to date. If you wanted to dig deeper (and have a budget), you could go out to the iso.org website and actually purchase the 27001 and 27002 documents. They are licensed to individual users, so they may seem a bit expensive (depending on what your budget is), but you won't find a better source of information than ISO/IEC. The ISO/IEC 27000 directory though and iso27001security.com sites are independent websites separate from the iso.org site that still provides some insight and guidance into how you might approach an ISO/IEC implementation.

More Resources

Other Frameworks
- COBIT (IT Governance)
  - http://www.isaca.org/Knowledge-Center/COBIT/Pages/Overview.aspx
- ITIL (IT Service Management)
  - http://www.itil-officialsite.com/
- Unified Compliance Framework
  - https://www.unifiedcompliance.com/

Risk Management
- NIST
  - http://csrc.nist.gov/publications/nistpubs/800-30/sp800-30.pdf
  - http://csrc.nist.gov/publications/drafts/800-30-rev1/SP800-30-Rev1-ipd.pdf
  - http://csrc.nist.gov/publications/nistpubs/800-37-rev1/sp800-37-rev1-final.pdf
  - http://csrc.nist.gov/publications/nistpubs/800-53-Rev3/sp800-53-rev3-final_updated-errata_05-01-2010.pdf
- FAIR
  - http://www.cxoware.com/
  - http://fairwiki.riskmanagementinsight.com/

If ISO/IEC isn't appropriate for your organization, I recommend you look at COBIT as an alternative. I also recommend everyone understand ITIL. Although ITIL is not a security framework but a service management framework, there are definitely parallels between the two disciplines.

The Unified Compliance Framework (UCF) is another resource that I mentioned that maps multiple regulations and standards to one another. I've seen a number of GRC solutions that subscribe to the UCF, enabling you to more quickly identify and implement controls based on that work that has already been completed.

I've got a few resources here from NIST and FAIR in the risk management category. Again, keep in mind that NIST is more qualitative, while FAIR is more quantitative. Regardless of which risk management framework you choose, you need a common language for discussing risk internally. If your organization does not yet have a common language for that discussion, start here. Take a look at those two.

Even More Resources

SANS 20 Critical Security Controls
- http://www.sans.org/critical-security-controls/

GIAC Certified ISO-27000 Specialist
- http://www.giac.org/certification/certified-iso-27000-specialist-g2700

Australian Department of Defence Top 35 Mitigation Strategies
- http://www.dsd.gov.au/infosec/top35mitigationstrategies.htm

Common Sense Security Framework
- http://www.commonsenseframework.org/

IT Security Career
- http://www.itsecuritycareer.com/

I mentioned the SANS 20 Critical Security Controls, a slightly deceptive name since these 20 categories contain closer to 150–160 specific control requirements.

If you wanted to become a certified ISO/IEC 27000 specialist SANS, then I recommend you pursue the corresponding GIAC certification.

If your organization is focused on breach mitigation, the Australian Department of Defence Top 35 Mitigation Strategies is incredible. It's a terrific resource that is not as widely known as it should be.

The last two resources are websites that I maintain to help share this information. The Common Sense Security Framework (CSSF) was designed to enable organizations to quickly assess the security of their third parties, as well as turn that lens inward to examine their own control set.

The CSSF contains what I consider to be the top three controls in each of seven key areas. If an organization does not currently maintain these 21 controls, then asking any additional security questions is a waste of both your time and theirs.

IT Security Career is designed to help aspiring information security professionals find open positions in the field because, again, I cannot over-state the importance of finding and employing qualified professionals.

Professional Organizations

ISSA (Information Systems Security Organization)
- http://www.issa.org/

ISACA (Information Systems Audit and Control Association)
- https://www.isaca.org/

SANS
- http://www.sans.org/

InfraGard
- http://www.infragard.net/

OWASP (Open Web Application Security Project)
- https://www.owasp.org/

If you've not had that field experience, there are multiple professional organizations that you can participate in to begin learning the ropes and to network with current information security professionals. ISSA, ISACA, SANS, InfraGard, and OWASP all have local chapters in multiple cities around the world, and you may find one or more of these organizations in your own city. ISC^2, which I don't have on the list here, is starting chapters throughout the world, so you may have even one more professional organization to consider.

You may have local organizations as well, organizations that don't have a national or international footprint. For example, in Indianapolis, Indiana, there is an organization known as the Indiana Security and Privacy Network (INSPN), this gathering of information security and audit professionals is very well-attended, and the information they share is very helpful to all those who attend.

CHAPTER *20*

Conclusion

I hope this book has provided you with the information you need to improve your information security program, and to take the next step in your career as an information security professional. I strongly encourage you to dig into the additional resources, to participate in local professional organizations, and do what you can to help us continue to secure organizations around the world.

Thanks much for all you do!

Printed in the United States
By Bookmasters